The Color Red

by
Julie Jurgens-Shimek

AuthorHouse™
1663 Liberty Drive, Suite 200
Bloomington, IN 47403
www.authorhouse.com
Phone: 1-800-839-8640

AuthorHouse™ UK Ltd.
500 Avebury Boulevard
Central Milton Keynes, MK9 2BE
www.authorhouse.co.uk
Phone: 08001974150

This book is a work of non-fiction. Unless otherwise noted, the author and the publisher make no explicit guarantees as to the accuracy of the information contained in this book and in some cases, names of people and places have been altered to protect their privacy.

First published by AuthorHouse 2/6/2007

ISBN: 978-1-4259-8835-7 (sc)

Printed in the United States of America
Bloomington, Indiana

This book is printed on acid-free paper.

Cover photo courtesy of Carlson Studio, Spicer, Minnesota; Marti Carlson-Twite

Bloomington, IN Milton Keynes, UK

authorHOUSE®

......for my Michael and all those like my Michael

Table of Contents

Michael and Dad riding Mary Lou, a friends horse, Summer 2006

Foreword

I have such vague memories of the day I was told my son had Autism. I can not remember where it was. I can't say whose office we were even in anymore. After meeting with such a vast number of people, through numerous appointments, they seem to have all been placed in my mind almost as though they are a dream. I can not remember whom it specifically was that told us. What I do remember is the word Autism, and the statement "there is no questioning it anymore, your son is Autistic".

I did not know I could cry like I did. I did not know when it was time to leave if my legs would carry me to walk to the car. My stomach felt as though I would vomit. I do not remember anything of the travel home other then the silence in the car between my husband and myself.

That night, again another night without sleep all I could do was think, now what do we do? After two and a half years of searching for that answer what I can say is you live, you move forward, you love your child, you laugh, you cry, you are at times angry, at times swim in self pity, you still wake up every morning and you are still a parent of an Autistic child. The sooner you accept that, deal with it and realize, the bills still have to be paid, you still have another child who needs you, and a marriage that needs to be treated like a fragile piece of china. That marriage, if you are not very careful with it may break. You learn, you read, you discover your child. Our son Michael at times can not be in the world we live in. We have over time learned how to step into his world.

It was many weeks before we shared with anyone our son Michael's diagnosis. It took almost a full year before I could say the word Autism and its content to my Michael without crying. Even now two years later, I can still cry thinking about my son and the challenges all of us will face over the course of a life time. Yes, I am passionate and emotional about Autism and my son. I am his Mother.

I began writing not long after Michael began going through a battery of tests to better determine what exactly it was we were dealing with. I found it a necessity as the constant questionnaires and the exasperating amount of paper work that I needed to fill out. Writing was the only accurate way for me to provide specific information that they needed. What I discovered was after an exhausting day with Michael, when sleep was all I could think of, taking the time to write actually made me feel better. And at that time, that was the only thing working.

After Michael's official diagnosis, I continued to write. What I did not do for well over a year was to sit and read everything I was writing. I never looked back it seemed.

In early 2006 the Federal Government declared Autism an epidemic. When I heard those words, I made the assumption that now this will make people stand up and take notice. Now, something will be done for our children. I have learned over the course of the last two years to assume nothing. The moment I do where it concerns Autism or my son, it always back fires. So many parents describe their entrance into the world of Autism as if someone snuck into there child's room one night and stole them from them.

Not long after the Federal Government made their declaration, I started reading my Michael journal. I was exhausted after I finally finished it. So many times while reading it, I would say out loud to myself "how did I get through that"? "I did such a great job at handling that problem". On some I said "one could not have done a worse job then you in handling that". Reflecting over past situations at times past crisis's concerning Michael, I was amazed at either how well I handled a situation or at this stage of the game how poorly I handled situations. It was good to look back at where we were, how far we have come, and our plan for where we are going.

What Is Autism?

What is Autism?

Because Autism is based on the spectrum of a range it is important to remember that no two autistic people are the same. When trying to describe autism in a definition term I feel like I am being too general in my description.

If you look at the Centers of Disease Control and Prevention's definition of Autism it gives not only a good overview it also provides some examples for easier understanding. I have spent countless hours on the CDC's website reading thousands of studies, findings and facts about Autism.

Autism according to the CDC is a lifelong disability characterized by repetitive behaviors and social and communication problems. ASDs include autistic disorder, pervasive developmental disorder-not otherwise specified and Asperger disorder. People with ASDs tend to have problems with social and communication skills. Many people with ASDs also have unusual ways of learning, paying attention, or reacting to different sensations. ASDs begin during childhood and last throughout a person's life.

Even though the definition is vague and sounds scientific I prefer theirs to others. I like that it provides an overview of some of the general characteristics but does not limit nor group them. My take on it is it provides a large area for interpretation and a lot of areas to "move around in". There is nothing basic about our Michael. I would have great difficulty if asked to categorize him in a basic definition.

To me Michael has classic autistic behaviors. He does not talk. He has repetitive behaviors at times. He is very specific and fussy on how things have to be. He functions best by a strict routine. He has sensory issues. He does not do well in large groups of people. He is easily over stimulated. He has food sensory issues. He is gifted in areas that are marked by intelligence. He also has not reached certain milestone that other children have reached or he has reached them however at a later age.

The area we have noticed that does not seem to have affected Michael is he loves contact with people. Small groups or one to one works best. Michael is very affectionate to his family and makes eye contact with us all day long. He recognizes our facial gestures and responds to a smile, laugh and at times a look of disappointment. Michael like most of us can be a little manipulative with others to get what he wants. At times he is a charmer.

Personally I think it is best to group autistic behaviors with a straight line with no real beginning and no real end. That way others behaviors can be added to either end. So much is not yet known about this disorder. I feel it is best to not limit any one issue or behavior with those that have it.

Educating and Obsession

When Michael was diagnosed, I had to force myself to read about it. It was depressing and I was hanging on to the chance that it just was not true and that someone would tell me it was a misdiagnosis.

Eventually, I accepted that I was kidding myself and that I needed to live in the reality of the situation. Once I did that, the obsession began.

I wondered just how much time I could spend on my lap-top before it would burn itself out. I spent as much time as I could spare reading, chances are if it was available via the internet, I have read it.

I encourage every parent who has an autistic child to read, read everything you can, some if the information is applicable, some not.

I eventually stopped reading all the scientific information as I do not hold a PHD in Chemistry, Biology, Genetics, nor am I a MD. I found myself swimming in a pool of information that I could not apply to day to day functions as a family.

I have passed what happened, who is responsible and except this situation as it is and have to move passed it. If not, I will miss even more precious time with Michael.

I found that I needed to hear about other families with Autistic children. I wanted to know how other Mothers and Fathers were coping. What were they doing for their children, how were their marriages, how did they manage to get through the day? What were their biggest concerns, their fears, how were their finances? What was their plan?

What I have found is almost nothing. I found a few books, some articles, and a few things in magazines. Why, I wondered? I decided many months ago, that I have something to say about Autism and it applications to families and I want someone to listen.

That is how this book came to be.

Michael and Mom

Strictly for Mothers

Being the Mother of an Autistic Child is like using the word "Snagglenegit" no one knows what you mean, or what you are talking about. You just have to experience and live it to understand it.

The moment I try to describe it, everything changes.

I am exhausted every minute of the day. I have a physical and mental exhaustion that almost paralyzes me at times. Like any mother, you worry about your children. Will they be healthy, happy, safe, educated, loved?

I too have those worries. I also worry about all of the obstacles that Michael and I will face together and separately.

Because Michael does not talk and seems to have a very high tolerance for pain, I often do not know if he is ill or hurt until the bruise or a fever happens.

I took him when he was about 3 ½ to the Doctor for a check up, the Doctor looked in Michael's ears as part of the exam. He looked at me and said that Michael had a serious ear infection in both of his ears and has had this for some time. I also got "the look" that I have come to recognize from people that I interpreted as the "you are a rotten and irresponsible mother" look.

This look to this day it hits me like it did the first time I saw it.

I worry day to day on the challenges that I face with Michael, both safety and my nerves. By the way they are frazzled most of the time.

I worry about what will happen to Michael when he is older, and Jim and I are gone or not in a capacity to care for him due to our age. I always worry, who will love my Michael when we are gone?

As Mothers, we are doers. What can I do for you? What do you need? What can I provide for you to make your life better? With Michael, he is not able to answer me. After an afternoon of screaming and tantrums and yelling at me, I often discover that all he wanted was a toy, or a movie, or a special shirt. My biggest obstacle with Michael continues to be communication.

I often think of it as having someone in the house from another country who does not speak English and has no way to tell me what they want, instead they just scream at the top of there lungs all day in frustration. I recall one day I was so tired of being yelled at and while Michael was screaming at me in frustration, I screamed back. I understood what he was feeling and why he was yelling and screaming all the time. The combination of a child who is demanding (as all children are) combined with no real way to meet those demands is a recipe of "insanity stew" at our house.

When I look in the mirror now, I move in close, I study my face, when I pull back and look at myself again, I ask myself the same question " who is that person" Since Michael was born, I have at times lost myself.

My life has become unrecognizable and consumed by questions. Most of them I have had to accept have no answer.

I will be the first to say that over the course of the last 5 years I have taken my fair share of time swimming around in self pity, blaming others for my troubles and finding excuses for not living my life to the fullest. Every now and again, it seems I need to revisit that feeling and swim for a few days, have some tears, talk out loud to myself and rant and rave. Now... before I let myself jump in I put on a life vest.

I have "do" rules for self pity that I force myself to follow. I am able to recognize when it is happening, and I give myself no more then 3 days. I'm sure to describe this seems so stupid and self absorbing. These are two of the words I rant to myself when I am swimming and need to get out of the water, stupid and self absorbing.

I have found that for me it is okay to be sad about the situation that we face with Michael. I often watch Michael while he is playing, and for him, he seems very happy and content with his life. That brings me comfort. He seems unaware that he is not the same as everyone else. I know communication is his biggest frustration. I believe this will continue to be an obstacle and one that will manifest itself into the ability to be a real anger and rage issue for Michael.

Often when I am introduced to someone, I want to say "hi, I'm Julie, occupation? Frustrated and frazzled Mother, living on the edge".

Ryan, Michael and pooches, Christmas 2002

Michael doing his ho, ho, ho, Winter 2007

Beds, Curtains, Drawers and More

A time comes for all parents to move your child from a crib to a bed. We found this not as a milestone, but as an obstacle. Once we moved Michael from the confines of his crib, we had huge safety issues. We moved Michael into a full size bed. He was older then most children when we moved him to his "big boy bed". We choose a full size bed as it was anticipated that one of us may have to sleep with him for some time, when I say some time, we thought maybe years.

Michael was unimpressed with the bed. Michael hates change. Any kind of change seems to put him in a tailspin. He cried and refused to be in the bed. After some persuasion, and Dad crawling in for several nights this went better. We also gated him in his bedroom with a baby gate. This however did not set well with Michael. Confining him was a need. Safety continues to be our top priority with Michael. We practice it diligently.

After some time of Mom & Dad staying with Michael in his bed he began to accept it. Unfortunately for Michael (I believe most young children) he soon wanted us in bed with him every night. We had to stop this as he would only then stay in his bed if one of us was with him.

After about six months with Michael in a big bed something happened. At times I try to figure Michael out. Why he does things. Good and bad. Just when I think I have figured it out, I realize I am wrong. No different then someone playing around in my head attempting to discover why I do things. Without asking the right questions and me giving the answers, the chances are they would be wrong.

One evening after tucking Michael comfortably in his bed, his famous boo cradled close to his cheek, his favorite movie of that day playing quietly on his T.V. his room comfortably dark and the house quiet to encourage a peaceful rest I went to check on him.

What I found stopped me in my tracks.

Michael small as he was had managed to take a full size bed, strip the sheets, mattress pad, pillow cases, blanket, and his bed comforter off the bed. The mattress and had been flipped to the other area of his bedroom. He was about 3 years old.

I was stunned. He stood there playing in his room, seemingly unaware that what he did was a big "no" to his Mother. I scolded him and said "no, no" and pointed to the bed and all the bedding strewed around the bedroom. I moved the mattress back to bed, no easy task for a 35 year old women, and remade the bed and tucked him back into bed and said "now you go night, night, and don't do that anymore. I gave a hug and a "smooch" to Michael. When I walked away from his room I was still bewildered by what had happened. Why would anyone do that? How in the world does he have the strength to move a bed mattress in a full size bed as I found it hard and cumbersome to do myself? Why would he destroy his bed? The questions puzzled me. I however continued on with my evening of household duties. Maybe twenty minutes later I again checked in on Michael. It had been so quiet I assumed he had fallen asleep. He should be tired after the work out he had sustained from the entire moving the bed episode. When I looked into his bedroom I was again shocked. Michael was quiet and still in his bedroom. I was amazed to see that the bed was once again torn apart and the mattress moved off the bed. Again I scolded and said "no, no, don't do this anymore" I put the bed in order and again tucked Michael into bed.

Over the course of several weeks that full size bed was torn apart by Michael dozens of times. It happened sometimes soon after he was tucked into bed and sometimes in the middle of the night. During these few months I was getting little to no sleep again. I was exhausted all the time. It seemed that Michael was having difficulties sleeping through the night also. He did not awake crying or screaming, just waking in the night. Most often he would eventually give a holler that would alert me to his being awake. I would go check on him and find the bed torn apart and the mattress again moved off the bed.

I was stressed out. Only Jim & I knew he was doing this. I chose not to mention it as I felt that it shed a bad light on Michael. I did not want anyone to question Michael's behavior.

One afternoon while my Mother was at our house, Michael did it again. She was surprised at Michael doing this and also amazed that he had the strength and determination to move his bed. She was firm with me and said that I had to stop this behavior in Michael. This was unacceptable. I listened and thought to myself; people tell you what you have to do with no real direction on how to do it. It made me feel again like a failure as a Mother. I know my Mother and her kind heart. It was never meant for me to take it in a way that made me hurt and sad, but I did. I believe as fragile as I am when it comes to dealing with Michael, I take things strait to my heart and it hits me hard. Like most situations concerning our children, it is easier said then done when it pertains to discipline and your children. It was so difficult for me to discipline Michael when he was younger. I had no idea what he understood and if in fact he could be held accountable for his actions with his disability. I could think of nothing more awful and cruel then to punish and discipline a child who has no idea what they did wrong or the ability to have known any better. To me it was abusive and the worst decision I could have made to would be to discipline him.

Everything changed one night. I was beside myself after days with Michael and constant behavior problems with him. Crippled with all of my minute to minute issues of safety with Michael I was exhausted. I was spending my days contending with Michael, my evenings doing my house duties that most would have handled during the day. I was up the majority of the night also contending with Michael. After months of this I was almost catatonic.

That evening within about a twelve hour period Michael destroyed his bed thirteen times. All I did that night was move the bed back and remake it on and off the entire night. I was at my end with this. I spent yet another night crying. The last time I went in to do his bed he giggled at me. It was at that moment I realized that Michael was well aware of what he was doing and was quite entertained. He loved all the attention he was receiving from me each and every time I came into his room and put his bed back together. This was the early morning hour that Michael received his first spanking from his Mother. It was not a spanking to cause pain. I do not believe he felt anything more then a slight sting through the pajama pant and the cushy padding of a diaper. This along with my voice raised in a tone that Michael had never heard sent him into a shocked state. His lip quivered and I put him into bed. I walked away this time, no hug given, and no smooch. I said "no more!!"

"You stay in that bed and go night". I walked away and went to the living room, sat in the dark and cried. I believe that night we both cried ourselves to sleep. The next night and for many months when I put Michael to bed I said "you leave that bed alone". It was many months before it happened again. Every few months he tears it apart. I believe he needs to test me once in awhile to see if it still is a big deal or not. Now when I scold him, he puts it back together. I believe the thrill for the most part is gone as it is not much fun to make the mess and have to clean it up. Hence: The bed that was a huge issue is no longer an issue. Once again…my Mother was right. I needed to take control.

The bed issue was one of many that we have had to deal with. As the curtains were being pulled off the mounting brackets and the holes spackled. I reminded myself of the bed issue. A good scolding and punishment ended that problem. Later it was all the clothes taken out of his dresser and thrown around, sometimes in the middle of the night. When his behavior reminds me of the bed issue, I handle it with discipline. Again for that moment the problem is solved. I no longer kid myself. I believe there will be issues for years, maybe forever of one kind or another. I am pleased I now have some tools to handle them. I needed to realize that with Michael's form of Autism he does understand a lot of things. He is in so many ways a typical five year old boy. He understands when he has done wrong. We would do a great disservice to him if we allowed him to behave in a way that is unsafe, or unacceptable. No one wants to be around a child with bad behavior Autistic or not. I know I need to provide proper discipline when needed to make his life better.

When I talk about this please understand that disciplining one of my children is harder and more hurting to me then to them. I hate to be tough with them. I often feel as though I am failing as a parent, being cruel and mean. I have though discovered that for us, and more so for Michael, life is better with guidelines and rules. He does better in structure and behavior to me is a form of structure. The way it was going around our house with the constant ciaos and going for so long with little to no sleep I was close I believe to having a nervous breakdown.

I have to remind myself that I am Michael's primary care giver. If I am falling apart so is everything and everyone around me.

Michael now makes his bed every morning before leaving his bedroom. When I think back to the way it was and where we have come, I just have to laugh and praise both Michael and I for getting through beds, curtains, drawers and more.

Michael, Winter 2007

Michael and a new super hero toy, Winter 2006

Safety

Just when I let my guard down Michael again showed me who was the boss.

When Michael was young, sleep.... those five little letters were something that was taken from me. I am not talking about the eight or nine hours we are suppose to get. I am talking about living on three to maybe four hours of sleep in broken time over a three year period. I looked and felt like the creature from the black lagoon. If I had been granted a wish at that time, for myself, it would have been to sleep. Michael slept in sporadic patterns and chances are felt as awful as I did most of the time.

This type of sleep pattern is not uncommon for Autistic babies and young children. Finally when Michael was about four years old slowly he began to sleep for longer periods of time. He did not do a full seven or eight but did do five to six. I had been so accustomed to this sleep pattern I had a hard time sleeping. Over a years time frame both Michael and I found some sleep. It is a rarity now that he awakes in the night. A secure solid baby gate in his bedroom blocking the entrance to his room was working wonderful at keeping him contained. Keeping him in his room coupled with a full nights sleep was a huge benefit to all. That was until one night when Michael was five years old.

When I went to sleep sometime around midnight the house was quiet. One husband, two sons and three hunting dogs were all sound asleep. For any mother there is a sound of silence that is welcomed at the end of the day. I love my late night alone time. I also am a junkie for old black and white movies and Larry King to lull me into a good nights rest. At three twenty in the morning I awoke to Michael standing by my head poking my nose and giggling. I was stunned for a moment and then sheer panic set in. I jumped up. Michael continued to giggle. He was pointing to the TV. I was half out of it trying to figure out what was happening.

I walked out to the dining room. The kitchen light was on and Michael had set up a Santa Sleigh and had toys all lined up. The light was on down another hallway and a bathroom light was on. I looked down the stairs and the light was on in the family room. Michael had been all over the house, as quiet and keen as a cat burglar. I noticed the time and scolded Michael. When I took him by the hand and walked him to his room he protested. When we got to his room the bed was made and his room neat and orderly. I put him back into bed and played a calm and quiet movie for him. I went to our sunroom and sat in the dark. Once again my stomach felt as though I would be sick. All I could think about was all the things that could have happened. Michael could have gotten out of the house. We live on acreage and along the water. He could have gotten to the cars in the garage. The possibilities are endless of the tragedy that could have happened that night. Our house is locked all the time. Several locks are on each door. There was a time I found comfort in that. However Michael is getting so smart on locks that I feel a time is coming soon when we will install a security system. Designed not to keep someone out but rather someone in.

I look at that little stinker and know he had to be walking on his tip toes. He was so quiet. I have no idea how long he was awake and on the loose in the house. It could have been hours or minutes. If he knows he is not telling. Later that morning Jim, myself, Grandma's and Grandpa's began brainstorming on a way to contain this little Houdini.

By the following day (Mom pulled the night shift that night sleeping with one eye open) a motion detector was mounted just outside of Michael's doorway. It has a wonderful range and is very accurate and the moment he steps out of his room an alarm goes off loud enough to give me a heart attack. I have been thinking of my seventeen year old, though sneaking out has not yet been an issue with him. This handy devise could have many possibilities.

On a serious side, I was again scared. I am always worried about safety with Michael. He has no fear and does not understand any type of consequences that can happen by his actions. We have had some scary situations and they will continue and many may be life long. I have to remind myself that when a crisis happens and the calm of the awful storm has lifted I do find humor. I always keep the serious part of this right in front of me but have to giggle at times when I look side to side.

Early last Spring the boys and Jim were down by the lake. Jim was burning brush. Ryan was playing with Michael. They were throwing the football around and chasing one another.

Some of the ice was off the lake but not all of it. The dock was out on the water and Michael ran as fast as he could for the dock. Ryan chased him and was yelling at Michael "no" "stop" as Michael kept running. He got to the dock and jumped in the lake. The spot he jumped in was not deep, just up to his thighs. Ryan reached down and lifted him up. Moments later Ryan walked in the door with Michael screaming. I came running. It was apparent that Michael was wet and mad. Ryan had this panic look on his face. Ryan said he just took off and jumped in the lake. Michael was mad at Ryan for bringing him in the house. I was mad at Ryan for letting him get in the water and not being responsible. When Jim walked in the door he explained that he had seen the entire situation unfold. He said they were playing so nice and that all of a sudden Michael took off like a streak of lightening and jumped in the water. He said Ryan did great in handling it and that if it were necessary they would have jumped in after him. Michael it seemed had no idea how dangerous a situation this was and had no problem being cold and wet and was mad when I put him in dry clothes, and made him stay in the house.

The summer before we had installed alarms on our house doors. When you come into the house you lock the door, lock the deadbolt, chain the door at the top and turn an alarm on. We are so accustomed to this it is effortless and strictly a routine. We do this for all the doors in the house. I realize that for some it may seem extreme. In Michael's case it is not. He has fantastic problem solving abilities. I am so grateful that even though we have all of these safety concerns we also have so many wonderful options for keeping Michael safe. The other thing I strongly recommend is to talk openly about your obstacles. I have accepted the fact that I can't be in charge of knowing everything. What I do know is that two heads are better then one and four are better then two and so on. I have at time been presented with an obstacle concerning Michael and others with ideas and wisdom have had fantastic solutions. Something that I have fussed about for days is a problem solved in the company of others. I also can say "if you try something and it fails, brush yourself off and try again. It does get easier".

The largest obligation/obstacle we face with Michael is safety. I believe this will always be the largest responsibility we have with him.

Communication, lack of reasoning skills, no fear, and no real understanding of consequences as a result of behavior will always be a huge problem to try and manage.

Michael has gifted areas. I have yet to appreciate his gifts to the full extent as they also come with huge safety factors.

Safety became an obsession of mine after two small autistic boys from different states drowned within a matter of weeks of each other. Both had wandered away and search parties had been looking for them. While researching these situations I found an article from a safety expert who talked about tracking devises that can be attached to people who are at risk. One trail led me to another and I found just the devise that was needed through my county Sheriff's office. It is called "Project Lifesaver" I called them immediately and they were out the next day. Michael now has a locator worn on his ankle that transmits a beacon similar to what wildlife officials have used to track animals in the wild. I found that the average person lost takes ninety minutes to find, if found at all. Between search parties, law enforcement, and air support the costs are enormous. The average time we were given was seventeen minutes before people are found wearing this type of locator once reported missing. I do not believe there would be a good outcome if Michael were lost for ninety minutes. Seventeen minutes sounds better in words but we all know it only takes a second for a catastrophe to happen. I just know this. If our Michael were ever lost I want him found. Period.

If you have an autistic child call your sheriff's office and see what they have. If they do not offer such a program contact you local hospital or nursing home for a trail to a private provider. The devise that Michael wears is also used for Alzheimer's patients with great results.

I have been told animals of high breeding have a microchip placed under their skin with a tracking devise should they be lost or stolen. I was also told that providing this type of devise for a child was cruel. Most often those with opinions like this do not have a vulnerable child. If this is ever offered for humans our Michael will have one implanted. Chances are the President of the United States has such a devise. If it is good enough for him it is good enough for our Michael. Always look at your options and be informed.

When Michael was about three, he developed a fascination with the bathroom toilets. If you were to ask Jim how many times he has physically taken the toilets out of our bathrooms to remove objects he may say in the area of a dozen times. A small bathtub boat, seven tiny reindeer over the course of many weeks, refrigerator magnets, numerous toys and things I am sure have just managed to get through the pipes. At one point I installed toilet locks in the bathroom toilets. While grandma was here watching Michael she needed to use the bathroom. She was unable to figure out how to unlock the toilet seat. To her rescue came Michael. He unlocked it for her to use and locked it after she was done.

Michael and cousin Amanda Shimek, Winter 2006

Michael, Winter 2007
Photo courtesy Kelly Shimek

The Color Red

One of the many traits of Autistic children is their fascination with color. On the other hand I know lots of children who are not autistic who are obsessed about their favorite color. I too, loved to wear yellow when I was a teenager. With Michael the color red is something he identifies with. It is a part of Michael's identity and the person he is.

I struggled for years to find the door that would lead me into Michael's world. For parents who still face the struggle to open the door to their child's world, I know the frustration and sadness you feel. Don't give up, chances are it will appear one day, unexpected, and your life with your child will change forever. There are many colors in the "rainbow of life" who knows what storm could make a mystical colored rainbow appear for you and your child. I have experienced the "pot of gold" at the end of our "rainbow of life". The treasure is magnificent.

To tell the story of the color red and Michael's fascination with the color red still moves me to tears. Parents of Autistic children, who have the same traits as Michael, will have a greater understanding when I talk about not having a connection with my child. For me, the first three years of Michael's life, I had no real connection into the world that Michael was living in. We tried everything we could think of. Movies, books, television shows, childhood toys, you name it we tried it, over and over. Still there was no connection. The color red changed all of that. Who would know that the combination of yellow and green would lead us into the world that my son lived in? We embrace the color red everyday, the color red surrounds us.

To set the story I need to go back to the very beginning, when Michael was six months old. My husband Jim borrowed a Santa Suit that a friend was not using for the Holiday's. I was surprised that Jim was going to dress up as Santa Claus, and that this was his idea. His Grandparents had recently moved into a nursing home and family was going to spend the afternoon with them. There would be a few young children there and this may "liven" things up for all.

When Jim emerged from our bedroom dressed as the "jolly" old man himself, all I could do was giggle. He looked so adorable. We were in a hurry to get to our family gathering. We loaded Michael up in his car seat. His eyes were "locked" on Santa Claus. I thought he may cry as he was looking at him so intensely. Assuming Michael was scared; Jim kept his distance as not to spark a crying jag. Michael's eye's followed Santa everywhere. Santa had a fun time entertaining friends and family that Christmas Season. The next Christmas the Santa Suit was unavailable, I was surprised how disappointed Jim was, the holidays came and went.

Over the course of the next year, Michael developed a fascination with Santa Claus. We bought books, videos, toys, you name it for him as he got so excited looking at Santa Claus. It was around this time that the color red made its entrance into our lives. Michael's fascination started out slowly, he was about two and a half years old at this point. He would choose the color red if it was given as an option, but if the option was not there, he let it pass.

The following Thanksgiving, Jim made a call to see if the Santa Suit would be available. Unfortunately, it was already booked for this holiday season. I once again saw the disappointment in Jim's face. I told him, if you are that bummed about not being Santa Claus, then let's get you a Santa Suit. He thought it was a bit over the top. I got the impression that it was fine to borrow one, purchasing one, stated he was acting "corny" or doing something that maybe his tough-old hunting buddies may give him flack about.

I started looking. In the mean time a "colorful aunt" came for a visit. Michael liked this relative as she arrived like a whirlwind and always had fun things in her purse and bags. She would tease Michael and chase him around. She always had fun shoes, often with high heels that he could stomp around in. One day when she arrived, she was in a Mrs. Santa Claus outfit. Michael froze when he saw her. It was close to Christmas and she had been entertaining a local Health Care Facility for their annual Christmas Party. Michael followed her everywhere. He touched her suit, it was soft velvet, he wanted her hat, and he wanted everything to do with that suit and her. I do not believe he saw her, only that red Mrs. Santa Suit. She had to take it off and hide it in our bedroom closet and we had to lock the door. He was obsessed with that suit. I believe that is when the color red took over our lives. I hold a special place for that Mrs. Santa suit.

After obtaining some information about where to buy a good Santa suit Jim and I traveled to Minneapolis, Minnesota to the costume shop. There Santa Claus was born into the Shimek family. When Jim walked out of the dressing room, now dressed as Santa Claus in the real velvet outfit with all the trimmings I realized as a young women in my thirty's that a chubby, gray haired, wire rimmed glasses kind of man dressed in red, could really "do it" for a young women like me. I fell in love with Santa Claus that afternoon. The store sales women stated that they had Mrs. Santa outfits and encouraged me to try one on. I did and needless to say we now were a "couple". As we drove home we discussed now that we have these suits, what are we going to do with them? It was three weeks until Christmas, and we had no game plan.

We snuck the suits in the house and hid them from Michael. We stared at them often over the next few days still not knowing what to do with them. It felt like we had a new car and did not know how to drive it, so we just looked at it in the garage and ohh'ed and ahh'ed at it.

We decided to take the leap, and visit some friends and their children. I went to the bedroom and began my transformation. It was extensive and exhausting just getting ready. When I emerged from the bedroom, Michael started jumping. He treated me as though I was the real thing. I was the women in red. I was no longer Mom, and he was fascinated with me. That was until Santa Claus walked out of the bedroom. To say that Michael went ballistic is such an understatement. He was done with me when the big man was around. He was not at all afraid of Santa, he just wanted to touch him, touch that suit, and feel that beard. Michael wanted Santa to hold him and carry him around. He did not want Santa to leave the room that he was in. Michael offered his beloved "boo" his blanket to be held by Santa as some sort of token or gift. When it was time for us to leave, Michael was very upset. He has over time come to know that Santa and Mrs. Claus leave, but they always come back. At the end of the holiday season I found a Santa Suit, red velvet, for Michael. Christmas is always on at our house now. The last July forth, Michael was wearing his Santa Suit in ninety plus degree weather at our house. Ho, ho, ho, is a phrase Michael attempts all the time.

We had four Christmas trees in our house last year. Michael fills our huge living room with a sleigh and toy reindeer for Santa to drive. We have discovered that taking it down at night only makes more work for Michael. When he wakes up and makes a new sleigh it gets more intricate and larger. He sits in the sleigh in his suit and hollers for us to come in and wave and do our merry ho, ho, ho.

Over the course of the next two plus years Santa and Mrs. Claus have entertained well over three thousand children and their families. We visit nursing homes, child care centers, and schools. We arrived on a fire truck for one of the surrounding towns lighting of their city's Christmas tree. That was followed with punch and cookies and a chance for the kids to get close to Santa and Mrs. Claus. We were a hit and will be back in town for the holidays again this coming season. Michael watched from the crowd with his Grandparents. He followed Santa the entire night. How precious.

The color red has now become an important part of Michael's life. He most often is wearing red. He loves red toys, and red cars, real or play. We have had on more then one occasion the road side problems while walking by a shiny red car parked by the side of the road. Michael just wants to touch it and stand by it. I have found that not all people want a four year old touching the new wax job on their shiny red sports car. There was a time I was embarrassed and apologetic. I have now passed that. People who own shiny red sports cars want to be noticed, and they want their cars to be noticed. I think this serves as a compliment that a four year old has taken such notice and for that matter has such good taste. I smile and move along when Michael is ready. For the joy that it brings Michael I am not going to fuss over a fingerprint left on the driver's door.

Michael lives with in a world of his own. I believe it is a world of beauty and kindness, laughter, and at times frustration. I watched Michael all the time, desperately trying to find a way into the place he lives. I now know how to open the door and join him. All I need to do is walk in a room he is in and shout "ho, ho, ho" and wave. The smile is instantaneous and often is followed with a replying "ho, ho, ho". That simple phrase and wave can become hours of contact within Michael's world. We can share a Christmas movie, read a Christmas Book, play with reindeer figurines, construct a sleigh, or color in a Holiday Color Book. Sitting with Michael in my lap while he is dressed as Santa Claus, sharing a moment together with my son in his world is the most beautiful place imaginable. It is a place I love to visit and am overjoyed each time he invites me in to this grand place, close to his heart.

I no longer believe that Santa Claus is a myth, legend or childhood fantasy. I believe him to be a real person, alive and full of joy and grand tenderness. I just can say, he also is my beloved husband. I also believe that one day, my son will be Santa Claus. Because he was born to be, and because he is real.

Michael at Sibley State Park

Our Child's Education

I was told by a Doctor that one of our many obstacles we may find might be in the educating of our son. We were told to stand firm, as education for Michael was the key in reaching his potential and that we needed to start now.

To say that this Doctor's words were correct is a huge understatement. We have obstacles. It seems as though they surround us. I feel like we reach and overcome one hurdle and before I can grab and enjoy the breath of ease another obstacle replaces it.

Unfortunately, when I talk about educating Michael it may leave a bad taste in your mouth. I still have that bad taste, every day it seems. No amount of brushing, mouthwash, or mints seems to make this bad taste sweet. I still remain with this bitter taste in my mouth.

If you are a parent of an Autistic child you need to educate yourself before you can expect others to educate your child. I stand firm on this. Educate yourself to the Education Laws of your state as each state is different. They may follow some of the same guidelines and all abide by the Federal Laws, but you also need to be savvy to your specific State Education Laws. I have learned that in the Law section of my son's education, we have dealt with a lot of criminals.

I spent one entire winter on my computer on Federal and State Education websites. They are very detailed and if given the time with repeated reading and searching areas for more information and clarification they make sense. As I stated I took an entire season to learn. I read, reread, I photocopied almost everything and combed over them with my trusted yellow highlighter. I marked areas I needed to research further and highlighted the areas I knew our school was breaking the law on.

I once read and believe this statement in its entirety. When you are meeting with persons from your school whose job it is to educate your Special Needs Child, you need to know as much about the education laws as they do, if not more. I took this statement seriously. I practice its advice all the time. I do a refresher several days before each meeting. It is not the job of your school to inform you of your Childs rights. It is your job to know them.

I have also walked away with this information in our particular case. People often do not do their job, nor do they always tell the truth. I also have found that people will throw you crumbs and expect you to eat them up and be happy to have gotten them, even though you are starving for more when educating your child. What I have found out is I should have swept those crumbs on the floor for the broom to clean up and asked for the big slice of cake my child was by law entitled to have and was suppose to have been given. I would like to say yes, we would like our cake and to eat it too! It is our son's right and it is the Law.

You will chances are have to "go to the mat" for your Autistic child for the rest of their life. The sooner you are willing to roll your sleeves up and if needed and take to the mat for your child the better the outcome will be. To say as parents when you have a child you have agreed to a huge responsibility is an understatement. If that child has Autism, you have taken on a responsibility of gargantuan proportions. I have at times taken to the mat for the education of my son. I now leave my sleeves rolled up at all times. I do not consider myself a problematic parent. I have yet to hear a member of our school say that I am wrong, or that they would expect any less if this were their Autistic child.

I have also had to accept the fact that I am not Superwomen. I can't fix everything. I also know that I can't accept everything. When the school repeatedly said to us that the money was not in the budget to offer Michael (and let's face it all the other Autistic children in our school K-12, who I gather their parents were also receiving the same speech) more, I felt bad, nodded my head and acted as though I understood. That was until I learned the Laws. At the time my son started Kindergarten our school was ranked #155 out of #166 schools in our state when it came to spending for their Special Needs Children and Special Education Department. Why did I not know that I wondered, right from the beginning? Something the school failed to mention to us in our countless meetings. Just the same old, we just don't have the funds. I have also come to realize, our school has funds, and they just choose to allocate them in different areas. Our Superintendent receives an incentive bonus every year. I am unclear what the incentive is suppose to be. Is it to be a Superintendent? Is it for him to continue to show up for his job? What? I have asked myself?

Our son Michael has had fantastic teachers. They have had the kindness and compassion that our family so desperately needed. Michael enjoys school, and I credit that to wonderful teachers and the paraprofessionals who work with him. I feel we have always had good relationships with his teachers. However, when it has come to the people in charge of our teachers, and the ones holding the purse strings per say, and the so called "directors" of departments, that bitter taste returns within an instant. I often left meetings with the feeling that I had the word "sucker" tattooed on my forehead. I stated in a letter written to our school board that we have been entrusted with this Autistic child. If we do not do what is needed for him, then we should not be allowed to have him. I often have wondered why a formatted letter pertaining to our son's education or lack there of written intelligently, with strong backing to our questions, concerns, and for that matter some complaints to seven board members, none replied. Does one believe if you just act as though it was not acknowledged there fore there is no problem, lest it will just go away?

We have become and will continue to be pro-active where education is concerned for our son. It is our obligation to him. We have no obligation to our school; they have one to our son. I believe kindness is deserved where it is received. I believe understanding is deserved where it is received. I trust little to no one, as it seems ulterior motives drives the bus often in the education of our son.

We had a member in the Special Education Department tell us that attending Kindergarten was not an option for Michael though he did qualify for our school Kindergarten program. We knew the law and their denial was a bold infraction of Michael's rights. The same member, in a later meeting, would try to turn this around by saying she didn't think we wanted Michael in Kindergarten. I will now bring a tape recorder to all meetings. Perhaps it will help people to be honest.

We were told at a different meeting that the school had approved funding for an Autism Specialist that would benefit several Autistic children. After tears overwhelmed me for I felt that we had finely gotten through to the school and that they were willing to follow the law and also were willing to make the investment in our school's Autistic children. Now, what they really did was to advertise for a Special Education Teacher. What they chose was a teacher with a degree in Special Education, with limited teaching experience and fresh out of college. I suspect this was done as the cheapest teacher is a fresh out of college teacher. I researched our states education laws. What our states constitutes as an Autism Specialist vs. what our school advertised for and subsequently hired as a teacher was like a compact car vs. a Ferrari. I am all for Special Education Teachers. Let's be realistic though. A Special Education Teacher maketh not an Autism Specialist. Again, we were served crumbs and at the time we gobbled them up. What we needed for our school's Autistic Students was that big slice of cake.

I remember that meeting like I was still there, sitting in the big blue swivel chair. What I will never do again in the presence of these people is cry. When we were told of the Autism Specialist I felt like in the matter of a fraction of a second we raced up and over that mountain we had been climbing for so long. The tears of joy overcame me. I began to cry, the type of crying where I was unable to speak. I nodded my head many times and mouthed the words "thank you" several times over. The tears I have for my son are a pathway into my soul. I no longer share those tears in the presence of someone who does not understand what each of those tears means to me. When I think of the tears I have shed in the five years of Michael's life, I believe I could make an ocean with their content.

I was raised in a home to be respectful of other people. I was also raised to not question people in positions of authority, let alone an adult. What I have found is that when I walked into that Elementary School. I felt like a kid again. I was in the presence of people of authority and I should not question them as it would appear as though I was being rude and disrespectful. What I now know and believe to be true is this. Michael has his own personal expert on his spectrum of Autism. It is me, his Mother. I am available twenty four hours a day for questions and am and will always be available for consultations to whoever has a question. I lost my voice when I was nine years old and my inability to speak and defend myself. With the help of my Mother when I was thirty seven years old, I found it only with her help. Find your voice as your child can not yet speak for themselves. You are the only voice they have.

Marriage

The statistics that I have found state that eighty percent of marriages fail when raising a child with Special Needs. This amazes me. If ever a couple needs one another it is at this time. Jim and I are determined and dedicated to each other, this marriage, this family and to Michael. I say that as I believe it with all of my being. Jim is my best friend and I his. I have been through a divorce one time already. I have no desire to do it again.

We have talked openly and are very honest with each other, I find that it helps. I have said many times to Jim, when our life is crazy, " this will be too much for our marriage to take." Jim has a grand sense of humor and is one of the most responsible people I have ever known. He takes each day in stride and reassures me all the time that things are fine and we are solid. We know that it will take both of us dedicated to each other first before we can do right by Michael. Jim has a wonderful way of walking in the door, taking one look at me, and knowing exactly what it is I need. Often it is a hug and for him to step in and be in charge of Michael for a bit while I get my wits about me.

It makes me feel good when family and friends say that we are perfect for each other and that Michael could not have better people as parents raising him. We celebrated our sixth wedding anniversary this year, however we have been good friends for ten years. We have been through more in six years then most couples go through in twenty. Our marriage is stronger then ever and we love each other more every day.

I encourage couples raising a Special Needs child to be good to each other. Respect each other, and always remember that raising a child, without a Special Need, also comes with challenges, just different ones.

We plan to host another wedding for our tenth, maybe sooner. We will do this to reaffirm what we already know. We love each other, and want to be together always. I wonder.. will I wear my wedding dress or my Santa Suit for the next one?

Jim and Julie Shimek also known as Santa and Mrs. Claus, Winter 2005
Photo courtsy of Carlson Studio, Spicer, Minnesota

Reaction

As parents we are naturally protective of our children. As a parent of an Autistic child I find I am at times overly protective of Michael. At times this is good and at times it may be wrong.

People's reactions to Michael are mixed. Before he was diagnosed people would just give "looks". Michael looks like any five year old little boy. This too has mixed blessings for us. Because he has no physical differences he is easier for people to accept. On the other hand Michael is and may always be very vulnerable. If he were in trouble or lost people would not look at him and recognize that he is in danger. If Michael had physical differences someone would know that he was in trouble and would intervene. If he were in trouble or lost he would not know it.

I have had many reactions to Michael when I say that he is Autistic. For most an innocent question leaves them with a blank stare and stumbling for words. I have found that most people are very curious about him and have a lot of good questions. I am always open to talking about Michael. He is a great kid and he is exciting at times for people to be around. It is always fun to have people meet him and see his many talents. Like any parent you are proud when your child does well. It is really fun when they do amazing things.

Some of the reactions to Michael have not always been positive. I have on many occasions had to take a person's foot from their mouth. They placed it there by saying something so wrong to a parent of a Special Needs Child. Loretta Young had a "swearing" box on one of her movie sets. Money was put in every time someone swore on the set. Paying money was a reminder to not do that. At times I would like to carry a " I say cruel and stupid things and don't even realize I do" box as a reminder for future conversations with uninformed people.

I love the movie 'Rain Man" I liked it the first time I saw it years ago. That movie imbedded an idea of Autistic people that may take a lifetime to change. Countless times people have said to me when hearing that Michael is Autistic "you mean like Rain Man"? I have had people make facial gestures mimicking what they think a person with Autism looks like.

I have had people suggest that we send him away to an institution. You name it and the chances are I have had it said to me.

I have bitten my tongue dozens of times with people who really had a piece of my mind coming. I am a rational person and I choose to not waste my time with someone so uninformed, and move along. At this time in my life so many things are pulling every ounce of energy I have. I am careful where I expend that energy. Wasted time and energy is time and energy I can not give to Michael.

I find the idea people have of Autism very interesting. Granted Michael has obvious talents in areas many do not that are directly related to his type of Autism. Michael is at times almost genius like. Our seventeen year old calls him a little Einstein and believes he is smarter then all of us put together. At other times I am so frustrated that he can do so many things I can't do but he is almost impossible to toilet train. I realize that many of our issues may work themselves out over time as he gets older. At times while dealing with insensitive people I want to say "chances are Michael is smarter then you and has a higher IQ then you did at 5 years old". I have remained able to control this as of now. For a few I may have to say it to them.

People often give the stand by " I am so sorry" response. I hate when people place pity on me that I neither need nor want. I often assume when they say this they are also thinking " thank goodness my children are fine". At other times I get the" oh" and they just stare at us. The ones I love are the people who engage Michael and ask questions. I have had a few people stump me on questions that I have no answer to or in an area not even I had given thought to. I love the people who see Michael for what he is, a five year old little boy loved by all those around him, he is different but not that different.

Our son Ryan who is seventeen is fantastic with Michael. Ryan often has friends at the house. His friends accept Michael and are amazed at some of the things he can do. I love when I am in the other room listening to Ryan and a group of his friends hanging out and they include Michael. They say things like " cool" and " he is so smart". It makes me smile and realize that at seventeen years old we have a lot of smart and kind people in this world. It gives me hope.

The Routine

People often wonder what our day to day life is like with an Autistic child. I wish I could give more detail on what it was like when Michael was first born. As I have mentioned, he just cried it seemed all the time. I held Michael almost always. With his constant crying I felt I needed to hold him close to me. Granted, with my oldest son Ryan who is not Autistic and was the best baby ever, I held him also almost all the time also.

I may have created a pattern with Michael, who knows? He did have his happy times when he laughed and giggled. I am reminded of this when I watch videos of him. I love to see my Michael at a time when I believed he was just like every other baby.

Our routines changed as Michael got older. He was a good eater when he was young. I remember feeding him in his high chair and he ate good, healthy food with minimal fussing. That is not the case now. Feeding Michael and providing the proper nutrition for a growing boy is not always a goal that we meet. He is very fussy about what he will eat. I believe this is due to sensory issues and the texture of foods.

We have some foods we know are a hit providing that he is hungry. Chicken patties that we buy from the Schwan's truck are his favorite. They are lightly breaded white meat only microwaved. Any other way and he will not eat them. They must be cut into small squares. I can hide small amounts of finely ground beef in spaghetti. This is his ultimate meal. Most forms of pasta he likes and will eat. I hate to say that Easy Mac is also a hit with him. I question the nutrition that he receives however his tummy gets full.

Blue bagged Doritos are a snack he loves and once he starts on them it is hard to get him to stop. Grapes and cut up apples are the fruit he will take but not in the quantity that I wish. Michael will eat peanut butter toast made only by his father. Anyone else making it is wasting their time. Sometimes Jim makes it for me. I know where Michael's coming from.

Chocolate or strawberry milk along with a strawberry yogurt are also some of Michael's favorites. He will also drink apple juice and orange juice most of the time.

Michael prefers to eat alone at the table or at Mom's desk while watching a movie. I have given into this or he does not eat. Whatever works to get the job done is how we handle most things. I most certainly handled Ryan differently when he was young, but Ryan was a different child.

Michael will not eat vegetables of any kind. I have tried for years and have accepted that it is not in the cards for him at this point. There was a time I felt that I was not taking care of him properly and ran the road of guilt about this. I love the quote from Dolly Parton in her 1992 movie "Straight Talk" " get off the cross honey, someone else needs the wood". Some may consider this to be too rough and taking a serious situation too lightly. I survive at times only with a sense of humor. Life is full of tears for some of us but you have to make room for laughter, often. I also remind myself that many parents may look at our situation, compare it to theirs, and wish they had the hurdles we have with our Michael. I think of that often.

Michael's routine at times is the same as most children. Bedtime is at seven P.M. as it takes some time for him to settle in for the night. A television is mounted on the wall of his bedroom. A calm Disney movie is put in. We now unscrew the light bulb at night as the temptation to get up in the middle of the night and play in his room is not an option when the room is dark. When we are having good sleep time he awakes between six and seven A.M. and starts the day in high gear when his feet hit the floor. He begins playing with whatever is the hot thing for him at the time. Right now as it is December and Christmas is in the air and Santa Claus surrounds him that is usually where he starts. We may have juice and whatever he is willing to eat while looking at Mom's computer. He loves to look at pictures of his super hero of the day or our trusty Santa. Mom will let him print out several for his folder and then we begin to get ready for our day and school. After this we dress. This always includes red in some part of his daily wear. At times he is head to toe red. Michael only has red jackets, and hats and shoes. We watch for the bus and grab our red backpack and head out the door. After a busy few hours at school he returns happy and still energized. A quick lunch and then off to play. Most often Mom still has her guard up and eyes focused in the back of her head. Michael is most often Mr. Mischief every minute of the day.

Dinner and then our nightly ritual of hugs, blanket, and picking up our toys leads us into our nightly rest that all of us need and deserve for the busy and at times stressful day we have had.

In closing I live by this: After a good nights sleep and fresh outlook life will be better tomorrow. Everything is a bigger deal and more upsetting when you are exhausted. My mother likes to quote an old saying "If you eat a toad first thing in the morning your day can only get better". I have days I am looking for a toad as a guarantee that our morning will be the only part of our day that will be hard to swallow. I will let you know if I ever try it and how it works.

"The Shimek Family" Winter 2006
Photo courtesy of Carlson Studio, Spicer, Minnesota

Update

I wanted to give an update of where we are now that this manuscript will go to print.

Michael is five years old. He is in a Kindergarten Program for Autistic Children and also does some time with his regular Kindergarten class. He attends school every day for four and a half hours per day. This is our schools first year with an Autism Program. I like to think that my persistence has had a hand in making this happen. I am sure many other factors and opinions were taken into consideration also. I do feel that our voice was heard. We have decided to embrace this program and his teacher who we have been very pleased with.

Even though I at times spoke harsh of our school and at times our relationship I wish to add this.

Our son Ryan will graduate from high school this fall. Ryan attends the same school district as Michael and has since he was in the seventh grade. Ryan has received a very good education within this school district. Ryan is not in any Special Needs Programs though.

I still have issues with certain departments within the district and still cringe when I have to contend with them. Trust is still an issue as even now when we have a meeting the first thing Jim and I recall are the untruths we were told. Once you lose trust and the truth comes into question where your child is concerned, it is difficult if not impossible to ever move beyond it.

In an article I wrote I believe last year I made a statement that I felt it was important when you criticize that you end on a positive note. I will practice what I preach and say this.

Michael is surrounded with teachers who have a passion for what they do. I believe when Michael meets a goal, they rejoice in that victory, as they should. I also believe that when Michael is stumped or is having a hard time or a sad and frustrated day they too feel it. I stand with my earlier words. We have never had any issues with those who teach Michael. We have a huge amount of respect for them and we try not to be difficult to manage. At times I think we have been successful at other times maybe not.

I have no regrets as I believe you have to speak up and be heard for the sake of your Special Needs Child. You are the only voice they have.

I understand that our government's current policies have created hurdles and obstacles for our school budget. I still have a voice and intend to use it when I deem it necessary. I am also going to contribute. Jim and I plan to make a donation in January to the Autism Program from our Santa & Mrs. Claus appearances. This has always been a volunteer thing for us. We will do this every year in the future also. We decided this year to ask those we make special appearances for to give generously. We realize that the funds needed for our school's Autism program is a substantial amount. We also realize that someone has to write the first check for others to follow. We are honored to write that check. In addition a percentage of the profits from this book will also go to the Autism Program. Again, someone has to write the first check for others to follow. I believe in generosity and stand by the fact that you have not given enough until you feel the sting. I told a man just the other day that you know you have given enough if when you sign the check you say to yourself "this is too much".

"That sir, I said is just the right amount".

Michael loves school. On weekends we still need to hide his jacket, shoes and book bag. He leaves with a smile and returns happy. This makes us feel good.

We have tackled several issues with Michael. Toilet training is one we are attempting yet again. Michael is willing when it is either of his Grandmothers, much better for his dad, and is often difficult for his mother. We understand that this is a mountain for many parents of Autistic children. I look at it this way. We will keep plugging away at this like any other mountain we have climbed with Michael. This one just feels like Everest and we will take it one step at a time with stops at base camp to rest and refuel. As much as we would like this mountain conquered we realize that there are many mountains out there and Everest is going no where. We may have to visit other mountains and return to Everest many, many times before all of us reach the top.

Michael is doing better at following directions. Mom has found her firm tone and he has a definite reaction to it. He also understands the upset face I make too with this tone. I do not yell. I am firm though. He hollers sometimes and yells at me to make me give in. I give in much less now then I used to as I know he can do so much more and he needs to do it for him not for me.

We recently started the up in the night routine again. Many days with less then three hours of sleep brought back the headaches and the haggard feeling I had for so long. I have no desire to revert back to this and have been trying very hard to get Michael back on track.

He is still always thinking and plotting. We continue to have our house locked up tight. We are making plans for the next step when we feel it is needed. He has become ever better with his problem solving abilities and getting his needs met this way. He still loves red & Santa Claus. He helped this year to decorate the Christmas trees and is in "full Santa mode". Televisions, VCR's, and DVD players are still an obsession. Chances are they will always be. He now has discovered how much fun the computer is. He loves to sit with me while on the web looking at pictures of Santa, Batman, the Joker and Star Wars figures. We look at hundreds and photocopy many. Michael loves to lay them out across the floors and just lay and look at them for hours.

I have many good days and fewer bad it seems. From time to time I put that life jacket on and swim around in self pity for a few days then eventually get back out of the water and move on. I still have tears even though I am predisposed to crying jags and it is my genetic make up. We cry for everything happy or sad or in the company of a stranger who is having tears.

My seventeen year old son said the other day " life is so hard Mom" I said to him " No one ever said it was easy, you will get out of a situation just what you put into it". I say many times to myself " life is not easy" and I hope that I am putting enough into it

Embrace the colors around you. Not that many years ago I was not fond of red. The color red surrounds me now and will forever. I love the color red.

Grandpa Ron Shimek and Michael

Interesting Information

At times talking with people about Autism I am presented with the same question. After having it presented to me so many times I now find the humor and have a giggle when asked.

For some when they ask or I tell them that our Michael is Autistic I am presented with this in response " you mean like "Rain Man"? There was a time I was offended, I now have to ask myself why that was? I enjoyed the movie "Rain Man" and was very entertained by it. Our Michael does not have the behaviors as the character "Raymond" from "Rain Man" as if he did I too would be on a flight to Vegas securing Michael's financial future in one evening at Caesar's Palace.

Bringing things back into perspective after hearing this so often I did some research on famous people with Autism, Autistic tendencies, Asperser's Syndrome, and people who are suspected of having Autism or Asperser's Syndrome in one form of the spectrum. I was surprised by some listed but not by all.

This is the break down of some of the information that I found.

Historical figures who displayed behavioral patterns associated with the autistic spectrum.

Hans Christian Andersen - Author

Albert Einstein-

Thomas Jefferson- US President

Michelangelo- Italian Renaissance artist

Isaac Newton

Andy Warhol

Alan Turing- Pioneer of computer sciences

Speculated contemporary figures-

    Bill Gates- it has been speculated that Bill Gates has many Asperger's traits.

Famous people with Autistic children-

    Dan Marino- NFL Quarter back for the Miami Dolphins

    Doug Flute- NFL player for the Buffalo Bills

    Sylvester Stallone- Actor

The list goes on for many with Autistic traits including many artists and gifted musicians.

The spectrum of Autism and Asperger's has touched many people we admire and respect and they have had an enormous impact on our society and culture.

There is a place for everyone and everyone has something to contribute.

Grandma's Perspective

By: Susan Jurgens-Kammen

I'm pregnant Mom! I could see the joy in Julie's eyes and hear the excitement in her voice. I knew she had wanted another baby since Ryan now twelve was born. An unhappy marriage kept her from that desire. Julie and I are close however I did not know the pain she felt in her marriage. She covered it well with a smile and an "everything is fine" response when asked how things were going.

She came to spend the last month of her Father's life with us. We were in need of help during those last weeks and she wanted and needed to be there. Mike and I were both so grateful for her help during those long sad days. She and I awoke to plan our day caring for her dad. Our plans changed daily as his condition worsened. Julie was a angel of mercy at the time of her Father's illness. The usual strong energetic fifty-five year old retired Minnesota State Trooper was fighting a losing battle with cancer. He wanted as few people involved with his care as possible. He was very capable of caring for his needs in the first two months but as the end of his life drew near I needed help.

Julie took the night shift with her dad. As I crawled into bed exhausted she and Michael talked for hours. They talked over everything. It was a two edged sword as they reminisced and talked about the end of his life. I would later hear from Julie that her dad asked if she was happy. When she did not reply he said "do whatever you need to do to be happy." I did wonder how she could be gone from her family for so long. I knew she missed Ryan. They were very close and talked often on the phone.

Her dad died in September and by November she was making plans to leave her husband. I worried about her and Ryan but Julie was determined to relocate. When Jim entered her life I knew she would be happy. He would love her, look out for her, and be a real mentor to Ryan.

Julie and I spent many happy hours planning the outdoor wedding. There were about two hundred family and friends there to wish them a happy life together. It was a lovely fall wedding. Julie was beautiful and Jim handsome. The announcement soon after of a baby on the way was not a surprise. She was thirty-three and I was concerned about her health. I was finished having children at twenty-three and although today's mother is often older I still believe younger mothers fair better.

I was in Mesa, Arizona for the winter and Julie and I talked everyday sometimes twice a day. She was uncomfortable as all women are and the flu became a battle for her for many days. Home in April, I spent time with her preparing for the new baby. We shopped for a bassinet, baby clothes and everything else a new baby might need. It was a particularly fun time as I now had more time to be with her. I had retired early and though I live two hundred miles away I could spend as much time as needed to help prepare for the new baby.

I was at their home about three weeks before the baby was due. As I left to go back to Grand Rapids I said, "You'd better have that baby soon. I don't think you can get any bigger." The next morning Julie was on the phone. She had a baby boy early that morning. I came the day she got home from the hospital. That little angel with auburn hair and the sweetest face was so welcomed into their home. I stayed for a week and Michael was a joy to hold and help care for. I had been a part of caring for many new babies and there was nothing different about this new little boy.

If ever there was a child who was loved it was little Mike. I don't think Julie put him down those first months. She cradled him in her arms and he loved it. I even called her once when I heard on the news that a new Mom had fallen asleep and smothered her baby in her arms.

I think she often said he cried and was fussy. I didn't put much stock in that. Babies cry and some have colic. A household's calm atmosphere is always changed by the arrival of a new baby and I thought Julie wasn't prepared for the real world of a new baby. There were seven children in my family. I worked two summers as a nanny when I was a teenager. I was used to children's antics and normal was not always well behaved.

Ryan was born to be good. He was a rare child with a gentle smiling personality and agreeable in every situation. He rarely cried, and was never fussy. He did not get into cupboards, rip things apart, or talk back. Nothing had to be put away as a simple "don't touch" was all he needed to hear. I know Julie never raised a hand to him and I don't know if she ever even raised her voice. She spoke in a calm voice and he always listened. This is how she believed children were and with Michael she had what I thought was a more normal child.

I saw nothing different in Michael the first year. He didn't crawl as soon as some children but the fact that mothers no longer laid their children on their tummies was a good reason in my mind for the late crawling. I did think it was strange that he did not attempt to talk. He seemed disinterested in people around him and was into himself. The doctor had assured Julie there was nothing wrong with his hearing. They would later discover a huge amount of water in his ears and tubes were put in. He did begin to respond more after that problem was dealt with. He now looked at you when you called his name and seemed more interested in interaction with others. He still however did not talk. I expected him to at least say the word no as he heard that so often.

No one wants to think there is anything wrong with a child. I was a part of the usual denial that most everyone sinks into when a problem is first suspected. Yes I wondered if Michael was different but pushed it to the back of my mind and assured myself that the doctor was right. Kids learn and develop at different rates and Michael was a little slow at some things.

Julie's stress and worry was getting more evident as the months went by. Little Michael was frustrated and mad. Some of his behavior was that of a two year old but the non verbal problem and the lack of understanding in some areas was staring us in the face and could not be ignored. Caring for him on a day to day basis was wearing and taking its toll on Julie. She suffered with bleeding ulcers and later hives. She had never had a good sleep history and her insomnia began to plague her almost nightly.

I had a new man in my life and was preoccupied with my own needs. Ken and I would soon marry and decide to move closer to both our families. We settled into a home on a lake not far from Julie. I have often thought of that as being a wonderful decision for many reasons. Yes we are closer to all of our children and my elderly mother and Mother-in-law. Julie however was more in need of us than I knew. I cannot say I know what to do in Michael's case but the more people involved in loving him and caring about him has to be better all the way around. I many times thought Michael needed a firmer hand and even to feel that hand on his bottom! We are all protective of our children. It is all right for us as parents to know our children's short comings. It is a totally different ballgame when someone else sees the faults. Julie knows I would never knowingly hurt her but her motherly instincts are on "attack mode" when it comes to Michael. Jim and Julie's hearts bleed for that little boy and he is so lucky to have them as parents.

Jim is totally supportive of Julie and a loving dad for Michael. He works long hours in the summer but is there to help with Michael in the winter months. Ryan is a seventeen year old now. He is six foot four inches tall and a strong football player. He is a typical teenager. Julie has probably raised her voice to him by now. He is kind and gentle with Michael when called for. He can also rough house with him. There is chasing, running, laughing, screaming, and tickling. Michael has a great big brother.

I like to shop for Michael. He is a cute little boy and Julie often buys tee shirts for him in the latest cartoon characters. It is sometimes Star Wars, Spiderman or Batman. It was getting close to school starting and I wanted to buy him some new clothes. I went to J.C Penny's and found him several shirts and pants one of which was a long sleeved red shirt with a small blue and white stripe across the front. It has since become known as "the shirt". He loved it and refused to take it off. Three adults have had to wrestle it off when it became too awful to wear another minute. He has taken it out of the washer soaking wet and tried to put it on. In most of his last year's pictures he has it on. As soon as I heard of the love of that shirt I went back and bought one more, the last one. They are too small now but sometimes he finds one of them and with his tummy showing runs around the house with a big smile on his face. Michael and I like to go shopping. As with all children he is better shopping with me then he is with his Mom. I bought him a Batman cape and mask. He slept in it the first night. Julie said his face was a little sweaty under the mask. She finally got it off after he fell asleep. He knows if he doesn't yell in the store he gets to have one toy before we leave. He carefully picks a toy. He may take several off the pegs look at them and put them back before he settles on that special one.

Michael and I get along very well. He likes to come here and visit and as with all children is better for me then for Mom. There are rules here too and I get a hard hug from him when I tell him no or have to scold him. He loves to watch movies and has his own television in the sunroom. I love to hear him growl like the dinosaurs. His grandpa Ken is his barber. Michael hates to have his hair cut but with clippers and a firm hold on him the job gets done.

I have shed many tears thinking about his life today and his future. I love him dearly but my biggest concern is for my own child, his mother. I remember the day Julie came over to my house laid face down on my bed sobbing and saying "what am I going to do about Michael?" I pulled her hair back and said. "It will be all right, you'll get through this". She said "Mother you always say that." I wanted it to be true, but I'm not sure I believed it at that time.

I think I am coming closer to accepting the hand that has been dealt all of us who love him. I ask myself often if I am sad for him or for us. I wonder if he will ever know what he is missing. I think not. The tears we shed are as much for us as for him and what we will miss. The life that we had planned to enjoy has been denied us. We had planned to go to ballgames and cheer him on, to a Christmas program at church, a graduation and someday a wedding. I feel life has cheated him and all of us at times. At other times I can say that God has a special plan for all of us and we don't know what his plan for Michael is. I believe that life takes twists and turns and eventually works out the way it is supposed to.

Julie feels overwhelmed by all of the problems that have come with an Autistic child. I think all parents want to do the right thing for their children. But what do you do when you don't know what is right? Where do you go and whom do you ask. I had no idea of the heartache that comes with a special needs child. Nothing can prepare you as a parent to have your heart ripped out and stomped on as you struggle to give your child what they need.

Our journey with Michael is just beginning. There will be sadness, frustration, tears, and joy. Laughter will also be in our lives as we watch him set up his Santa sleigh, line up the spoons for the reindeer, or listen to the giggles when he watches a movie. He has come into our lives and it will change us forever.

Acknowledgements

I wish to take a moment to extend my appreciation and gratitude to so many people who have been a part of my life and have offered guidance. With out their wisdom and strength I would not be the person I am today nor the mother that I am for always. Our family is blessed to have you close to our hearts.

Forever grateful,

Julie

My Father Michael, he still guides me everyday though he is gone. I miss our long talks and wisdom you gave so often. I have often thought of the big hug I have needed from you at times while dealing with all of this. At times I feel your hands on my sholders when I need the comfport.

My Mother Susan, she was instrumental is this book and in my life. I am lucky to be able to laugh and cry with a dear friend who is also my Mother. You have provided by example wonderful tools on being a Mother.

Jim, my dear friend, beloved husband and proud father to our boys. I love you more each day and can not think of who better to be teamed with while raising Michael. Your one "hot Santa" in my book.

Ryan, I was blessed with you many years ago, Michael is so lucky to have you as his big brother. I am so proud of you. You will be a fantastic father one day.

Michael, My Michael… held close to me forever. You have taught me the real meaning of kindness given freely. You are my gift that is at times wrapped in a puzzling package with a bright shiny red bow on top eagerly awaiting to be opened.

Ken, thank you for your kindness to our family and your love for my Mother.

Grandmother Sylvia, I aspire to be like you. Nothing tops a childhood memory then time with a fantastic grandmother.

Godmother to our Michael, Theresa, when so many fled you came running even more. You have often by example helped me to embrace new things. I am trying to not be so much of a princess.

Paul P. the picture in the dictionary next to the word friend. We are blessed to have you in our lives. As Jim's closest friend you excepted me from the start. I also love that we can tease each other like we do. Thank you for being you.

Ron & Mary, thank you for Jim. Your kindness to me has at times been overwhelming. Michael is so lucky for grandma and "papa" . Someday I believe he will say it Ron. I am proud and honored to be a Shimek.

To all of our loved one who keep us close to their hearts. We are thankful for all of your blessings.

Jeff, Linda, Jessica and Christa, friendship, kindness, and Godparents to our Michael. You never fled and have always been there. It means more then you know.

To Greg & Paul A, thank you for your generous time and wisdom.

For Marti Carlson-Twite from Carlson Studio, Inc. Your talents as a photographer are endless. You discovered and captured from our hearts with your vision what is the true meaning in photos of *The Color Red.*

To all of those who are a part of Michael's life. His teachers I commend on their patience and talents.

Life is...truly lead by those who teach.

Resources

These are some good areas for information , this is only a small piece of the cake of the information that is out there.

Autism Society of America
www.autism-society.org

Autistics.org
www.autistics.org

Autism Web
www.autismweb.com

Cure Autism Now: Home Page
www.cureautismnow.org

Autism Society of Minnesota
www.ausm.org

Centers for Disease Control and Prevention
www.cdc.gov

Their are many website specified through specific states. I listed a few from Minnesota's as I reside in Minnesota. Check out your specific state and see what is available.

Again I strongly encourage that you read about autism and read all you can. You will find what information applies to your situation. There is a fantastic genera of information out there. Knowledge is power. I found that once I educated myself on autism it was not as overwhelming or scary to me.

Michael 2007

Michael 2007

Sources

Centers of Disease Control and Prevention- Autism information

What is Autism?

Mauk JE, Reber M, Batshaw ML. Autism and other pervasive developmental disorders (4th edition). In: ML Batshaw, editor. Children and disabilities. Baltimore: Paul H. Brookes; 1997.

Powers MD. What is Autism? In: MD Powers, editor. Children with autism: a parent's guide 2nd edition. Bethesda, MD: Woodbine House: 2000. Pp 1-44. Date: June 27, 2006

Content source: National Center on Birth Defects and Developmental Disabilities

Author photo courtesy of Joseph Shimek

Author Information

Julie Jurgens-Shimek is a freelance writer. She primarily writes in the areas of Autism, Special Needs Children, Education and has a passion for Politics.

She is married and the mother of two sons. One who is Autistic. She lives outside a quaint little town in Minnesota on several acres of land along the Crow River with her family and their beloved hunting dogs Kojack, Hunter, and Gunner.

Printed in the United States
83617LV00002B